CONTENTS

CRAZY QUESTS

People have always wanted to do great things. People in ancient times built Stonehenge and the Great Pyramids of Giza. Later on brave adventurers crossed oceans to explore the world. The drive to do great things still exists today. People build skyscrapers and send robots to Mars. Artists, musicians, athletes and others are honoured for their amazing accomplishments.

But sometimes people don't need to do great things to achieve recognition. Whether they're the world's tallest person or have the world's longest tongue, some people are born to be record holders. Others often do wild and crazy things to set records. They may ride a lawn mower across the country. They might pull cars using only their hair. Or they try to solve Rubik's Cubes while running marathons. These people usually aren't famous. But their record-breaking achievements set them apart as the very best at what they do.

EDGE BOOKS

LIBRARY OF WEIRD

THE WORLD'S
CRAZIEST
RECORDS

by Suzanne Garbe

Raintree is an imprint of Capstone Global Library Limited, a company incorporated in England and Wales having its registered office at 7 Pilgrim Street, London, EC4V 6LB – Registered company number: 6695582

www.raintree.co.uk
myorders@raintree.co.uk

Text © Capstone Global Library Limited 2015
The moral rights of the proprietor have been asserted.

ISBN 978 1 4062 9208 4
18 17 16 15
10 9 8 7 6 5 4 3 2 1

British Library Cataloguing in Publication Data
A full catalogue record for this book is available from the British Library.

Editorial Credits
Aaron Sautter, editor; Kyle Grenz, designer; Charmaine Whitman and Katy LaVigne, production designers; Pam Mitsakos, media researcher; Kathy McColley, production specialist

Photo Credits
Alamy: ZUMA Press, Inc., 17; Getty Images: Science Source, 7, Photodisc, 29; Landov: Reuters/INA FASSBENDER, 27; Newscom: ZUMAPRESS.com/UPPA/Sue Andrews, 11, ZUMA Press/Ricky Bassman, 19, REUTERS/ALADIN ABDEL NABY, 4–5, ZUMAPRESS.com/Panoramic/Vukicevic, 12, Zuma Press/ UPPA, 13, Photoshot/UPPA/Charlotte Wiig, 9, Supplied by WENN.com/CB2/ZOB, 18, 24–25, ZUMAPRESS, 23; Shutterstock: Carlien Beukes, 28, Cidepix, 26, Hurst Photo, 22, Philip Lange, 21, Wayne0216, back cover; Wikimedia: Krish Dulal, 6, Maria Leijerstam, cover, 15, NASA, 14

Design Elements
Shutterstock: AridOcean, KID_A (throughout)

Direct Quotation
page 12: from "Skydiver Felix Baumgartner Breaks Sound Barrier" by Jonathan Amos for BBC News, Oct. 14, 2012. http://www.bbc.com/news/science-environment-19943590

Printed and bound in China.

Ashrita Furman knows a few things about setting records. Since 1979 he has set 532 world records! Furman is also the current record-holder for holding the most Guinness World Records at one time with 189 records!

Furman is just one of thousands of people who've pursued some of the world's craziest records. Read on to learn about some of the craziest stunts and wildest records ever achieved.

CHAPTER 1
THE HUMAN BODY

Some people are born with extraordinary bodies. They might have extra fingers, stretchy skin or an extremely long tongue. Other people are born with average bodies but turn them into something extraordinary. Have a look at some of the strangest human body records from around the world.

SHORTEST PERSON

Chandra Bahadur Dangi of Nepal is only 54.6 centimetres tall. He was awarded the world record at the age of 72. Three of his siblings are also less than 122 cm tall. However, Dangi also has four other siblings of average height.

HEAVIEST VEHICLE PULLED BY HAIR

In 2012 Asha Rani pulled a bus weighing 12,101 kilograms. That's two times the weight of an elephant! But that's not the most amazing part. Instead of using her hands, she used her hair! Rani put her hair into two plaits, then tied a rope from the plaits onto the bus. She pulled the bus more than 17 metres. Rani earned the nickname "Iron Queen" for her amazing achievement.

TALLEST PERSON

Robert Pershing Wadlow of Illinois, USA was the tallest man in history. He measured 2.7 metres tall. Wadlow was already more than 1.8 metres tall when he was 8 years old. His height was the result of a disorder in his **pituitary gland**. Wadlow was so tall that he needed special braces to help him walk. In 1940 Wadlow died at just 22 years old. He died as a result of an infected blister caused by one of his leg braces.

pituitary gland *organ that influences many functions in the body, including bone growth*

LONGEST EAR HAIR

Long ear hair is **genetic** and is usually only found in men. It's also more common in elderly people. India's Anthony Victor holds the current world record for the longest ear hair at 18 centimetres long.

genetic *relating to physical traits or conditions passed down from parents to children*

TALLEST MOHAWK

Japanese fashion designer Kazuhiro Watanabe holds the record for the world's tallest mohawk. It takes an entire bottle of gel and three cans of hairspray to hold its height of 113.5 centimetres. Watanabe let his hair grow for 15 years to set this record. When it's not in a mohawk, his hair reaches down to his knees.

LONGEST TONGUE

Stephen Taylor from Coventry has the longest tongue in the world. It measures 9.8 centimetres from the top of his upper lip to the tip! The length of an average tongue is only 2 centimetres long. Taylor exercises his tongue every day to keep it flexible. It's so long that it gives him a **lisp**.

lisp *speech problem that causes a person to incorrectly pronounce certain letters, especially "S" and "Z"*

LONGEST FINGERNAILS

Shridhar Chillal of India had the longest fingernails ever measured on a single hand. His nails grew to an amazing length of 6.2 metres! He began letting his nails grow in 1952 and didn't cut them off until 2000.

MOST WORLD BEARD AND MOUSTACHE CHAMPIONSHIP TITLES

The World Beard and Moustache Championships are held in various locations every year. The contest gives awards for more than 15 different types of beard and moustache styles. Karl-Heinz Hille of Germany has won eight titles at the World Beard and Moustache Championships.

CHAPTER 2
ATHLETIC FEATS

Sports fans can probably name several of their favourite professional athletes. But not all great athletes participate in major sports seen on TV. Some record-holding athletes have much more unusual accomplishments!

A RECORD SWIM

Swimming in the sea between the USA and Cuba is dangerous. Swimmers here risk being attacked by sharks, jellyfish and other dangerous creatures. In 2013 Diana Nyad became the first person to swim from Cuba to Florida without a shark cage. She first attempted the crossing at age 29 but didn't succeed until her fifth attempt at the age of 64. It took Nyad almost 53 hours to complete the journey.

SHOOTING FROM THE FEET

In 2013 Inka Siefker hit a balloon at the centre of a target with an arrow. But the amazing part is that she did it with her feet! As Siefker balanced on her hands, she used her feet to shoot the arrow a record 6 metres.

DRIBBLING INTO THE RECORD BOOKS

During a 24-hour period in 2001, Suresh Joachim dribbled a basketball for a record 156.7 kilometres. Joachim holds the second-highest number of world records after Ashrita Furman. Joachim's other records include the longest times for watching movies, shaking hands, bowling, drumming and playing in a band.

A PUZZLING RUNNER

In 2011 Uli Kilian ran the London Marathon to help raise money for cancer research. He also wanted to set a crazy world record while doing it. As he ran he solved a record 100 Rubik's Cube puzzles in just under 5 hours.

HIGHEST BICYCLE TIGHTROPE CROSSING

Acrobat Nik Wallenda rode a bike across a tightrope 72.5 metres in the air. That's more than 20 stories high! He held a 9-metre-long pole to help him balance. Wallenda also holds the record for being the first person to walk on a tightrope across the Grand Canyon in Arizona, USA.

GREATEST FREE FALL DISTANCE

Skydiver Felix Baumgartner made history in 2012. He jumped from a balloon 38.6 kilometres above Earth. Baumgartner was in **free fall** for nearly 4 ½ minutes before using his parachute. "When I was standing there on top of the world, you become so humble," he told reporters after his achievement. "You don't think about breaking records anymore … the only thing that you want is to come back alive."

DEEPEST FREE IMMERSION DIVE

Free **immersion** divers travel deep underwater without oxygen tanks. As they dive they can use only a rope to help pull themselves along. Austrian diver Herbert Nitsch holds the record for the deepest free immersion dive of 120 metres.

acrobat *person who performs gymnastic displays that require great skill*

free fall *descend through the atmosphere for a time without the aid of a parachute*

immersion *fully submerged underwater*

FIRST MANNED SOLAR-POWERED FLIGHT

The first manned flight using **solar** power occurred in California, USA on 18 May 1980. The pilot was 13-year-old Marshall MacCready. The small plane weighed just 31 kilograms. MacCready's father founded the company that built the plane.

LONGEST LAWN MOWER RIDE

From 2000 to 2001 American Gary Hatter rode his lawn mower for 23,488 kilometres. He travelled through 48 US states as well as through parts of Mexico and Canada. Hatter's lawn mower only went about 14.5 kilometres an hour. It took him more than eight months to complete the trip.

FIRST BIKE RIDE TO THE SOUTH POLE

Few people visit the South Pole – and even fewer get there on their bikes! In December 2013 Maria Leijerstam competed in the White Ice Cycle Expedition. Three people competed in this bicycle race across Antarctica to the South Pole. By winning the race, Leijerstam became the first person to ride a bike to the South Pole. Leijerstam's approach was unique. Rather than a traditional two-wheeled bike, she rode a three-wheeled **recumbent** bicycle. The race covered 637 kilometres in 10 days.

solar *to do with the sun; powered by the sun's energy*

recumbent *position in which a person leans back with his or her legs stretched out in front*

15

CHAPTER 3
ANIMAL ACCOMPLISHMENTS

Human beings love to set new records. But animals often achieve wild feats too. Some animals set records for their natural abilities. Others set records for things they have been trained to do. Have a look at some of the world's most incredible animal accomplishments.

LOUDEST PURR BY A CAT

Smokey was a loud cat! On 25 March 2011, this grey cat from Northampton set the record for the world's loudest purr. At 67.7 **decibels** Smokey's purr was almost as loud as a vacuum cleaner!

decibel unit for measuring the volume of different sounds

MOST TENNIS BALLS IN A DOG'S MOUTH

Many dogs love to play with tennis balls. Most dogs only carry one ball in their mouths at a time. But a dog from Texas, USA called Augie carried many more. In 2003 the golden retriever gathered and held a total of five tennis balls in his mouth at once.

MOST MILK FROM A COW

Smurf the cow lives on La Ferme Gillette farm in Canada. In 2012 she broke the record for milk production. During her lifetime Smurf has produced more than 215,768 litres of milk. That's about six times more than the average cow produces during its lifetime.

LONGEST SKATEBOARDING DISTANCE BY A GOAT

In 2012 Melody Cooke's pet goat, Happie, jumped onto a skateboard. It wasn't long before Happie became a world record holder. She rode the skateboard for 36 metres. Many people were surprised, but Cooke wasn't. She said that Happie often performed tricks like a dog.

WORLD'S SHORTEST DOG

The shortest dog in the world is a tiny Chihuahua called Miracle Milly. This pocket-sized pooch stands at just 9.7 centimetres tall! Milly lives with her owner, Vanesa Semler, in Puerto Rico.

WORLD'S RICHEST PET

The world's wealthiest pet is a dog called Gunther IV. When German Countess Karlotta Lieberstein died in 1992, she left more than £233 million to her beloved German Shepherd, Gunther III. Then after he died, the fortune was passed on to one of his puppies, Gunther IV. The dog's fortune includes several homes such as the former Miami mansion of singer Madonna and a villa in the Bahamas.

MOST NUMBERS IDENTIFIED BY A HORSE

Karen Murdock has trained her horse, Lukas, to recognize numbers. Murdock places numbers from one to five on a board in front of the horse. Lukas then uses his nose to point to a number after Murdock calls it out. In 2010 Lukas correctly identified 19 numbers in one minute as Murdock read them out.

LONGEST CAT HAIR

Before he died in 2014, Colonel Meow had hair that was 23 centimetres long. Owners Anne Marie Avey and Eric Rosario of Washington, USA, groomed him two to three times a week. Colonel Meow was a Himalayan-Persian mix. Persian cats are known for having especially long hair.

CHAPTER 4

MAN-MADE CREATIONS

What do an enormous whoopee cushion, a car made of cake and an underwater hotel have in common? They're all record-breaking objects made by incredibly creative people. Let's discover some of the most incredible and bizarre things people have made around the world.

FIRST UPSIDE-DOWN SHOP

Fashion designers Viktor Horsting and Rolf Snoeren don't just make unique clothes. They also built a one-of-a-kind shop to show off their clothing creations. From 2005 to 2008, they ran a shop in Milan, Italy, that was decorated to look as though it was upside down. The ceiling was covered with wood flooring. Mirrors were put high-up on the walls. Columns that should have started on the floor hung from the ceiling instead!

HAIRIEST CAR

In 2010 Italian hair artist Maria Lucia Mugno won the prize for the world's hairiest car. The Fiat 500 is covered with 100 kilograms of hair. Mugno used natural human hair to make her hairy creation.

WORLD'S TALLEST BUILDING

The Burj Khalifa building in Dubai, United Arab Emirates, is the tallest in the world. At 828 metres, it has more than 160 floors. It has an outdoor observation deck that's the highest in the world. The giant building includes apartments, office space, hotel rooms, a fitness club and underground parking for 3,000 cars. It is more than twice as tall as the Empire State Building in New York, USA.

WORLD'S NARROWEST HOUSE

One home in Warsaw, Poland, is less than 0.9 metres wide at its narrowest point. It was built in a narrow space between two tall buildings. The refrigerator can only hold two drinks. The dining room table can only seat two people. And the bedroom can only be reached by a ladder!

WORLD'S TALLEST LEGO® TOWERS

In 2013 a group of students from Delaware, USA, spent the summer building the world's tallest LEGO® tower. It measured 34.4 metres high and contained more than 500,000 bricks! Not to be outdone, childen in Budapest, Hungary, helped build an even taller tower in 2014. The new record holder stands at an amazing 34.7 metres high. Both towers were built in small sections and put together with the help of cranes.

WORLD'S LARGEST WHOOPEE CUSHION

Steve Mesure created the world's largest whoopee cushion. It has a **diameter** of 3.1 metres. It was made for the 2008 Street Vibe Festival of Sound held in London. The festival explored the role of science and engineering in making music and sound.

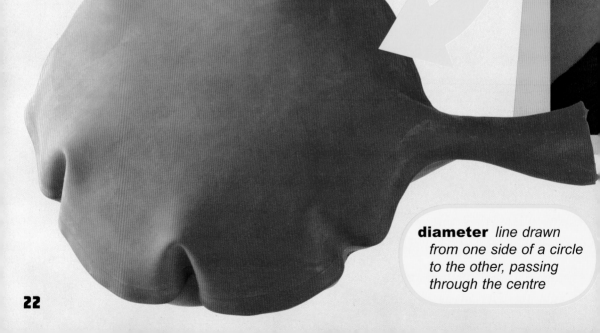

diameter *line drawn from one side of a circle to the other, passing through the centre*

FIRST UNDERWATER HOTEL

Built in the 1980s, Jules' Undersea Lodge in Florida, USA, delivers exactly what its name promises. To reach the hotel, guests must dive 6.4 metres under the sea. Despite the unusual entry point, the hotel has all the comforts of a normal hotel. It has hot showers, TVs and even a pizza delivery service. However, guests must be certified scuba divers to stay here.

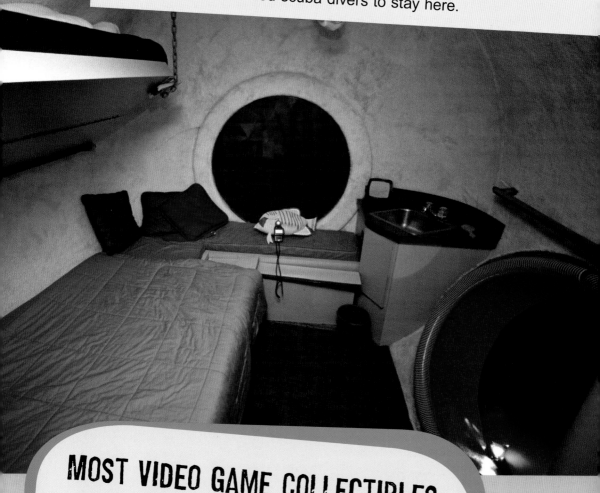

MOST VIDEO GAME COLLECTIBLES

Brett Martin has the largest collection of video game merchandise in the world. He owns 8,030 video game-related items. His collection is thought to be worth more than £60,000. The collection includes toys, figurines, controllers, stuffed animals, clothing and many other objects. Martin even has a set of Mario-themed power tools!

WORLD'S LARGEST WALKING ROBOT

The largest walking robot in the world is a 15.5-metre-tall dragon. The radio-controlled robot has a 12.2-metre wingspan and walks on four legs. It even breathes fire! German company Zollner Elektronik built the robot dragon for an annual festival in Furth im Wald, Germany. The festival includes a play about a dragon invading the town, which has been performed there for over 400 years.

LONGEST MOTORCYCLE

In 2011 Colin Furze from Lincolnshire built the world's longest motorcycle. It's 22 metres long and can carry up to 25 people. Its top speed is 56 kilometres an hour. However, the motorcycle is so big and heavy that it's very difficult to steer.

FASTEST SOFA

Glenn Suter holds the record for the world's fastest sofa. The crazy motorized contraption has reached speeds of up to 163 kilometres an hour. The sofa even has a coffee table attached to it!

FASTEST EDIBLE CAR

In 2012 Carey Iennaccaro designed, built and drove the world's fastest **edible** car. Ninety-five per cent of it was made from cake! The frame, brakes, seat and tyres were all real. But nearly everything else on the car could be eaten. Even the helmet Iennaccaro wore was made of chocolate and sugar. The edible car could reach a top speed of 17.2 kilometres an hour.

edible *able to be eaten*

CHAPTER 5

WEIRD ACHIEVEMENTS

Some world records are awe-inspiring. Some are unbelievable. And others are just really weird. One person set a record for burping! Another group of people set a record for brushing each other's teeth! Let's see what other really strange records people have achieved ...

HEAVIEST WEIGHT LIFTED BY A TONGUE

In 2008 Thomas Blackthorne lifted an object weighing 12.5 kilograms – using only his tongue! Before achieving the record, he had been lifting weights with his tongue for about 10 years.

MOST FEET AND ARMPITS SNIFFED

The Dr. Scholl's company is known for making foot care products. Employee Madeline Albrecht used to conduct research for the company. During her 15 years at Dr. Scholl, Albrecht sniffed approximately 5,600 feet and countless armpits.

FASTEST TIME ENTERING A SUITCASE

In 2009 professional **contortionist** Leslie Tipton zipped herself into a suitcase in just 5.43 seconds. Tipton started bending and twisting her body at the age of 22. She admired the flexibility and training of acrobats who could bend their bodies in odd ways.

contortionist
entertainer who twists his or her body into strange positions

LONGEST BURP

Italian Michele Forgione was responsible for the world's longest burp in 2009. The epic belch lasted an amazing 1 minute and 13 seconds!

MOST PIERCINGS

With 453 body piercings, Rolf Buchholz of Germany has more piercings than anybody else in the world. He has more than 100 piercings on his face alone! Rolf is also a big fan of tattoos. His whole body is covered in tattoo art.

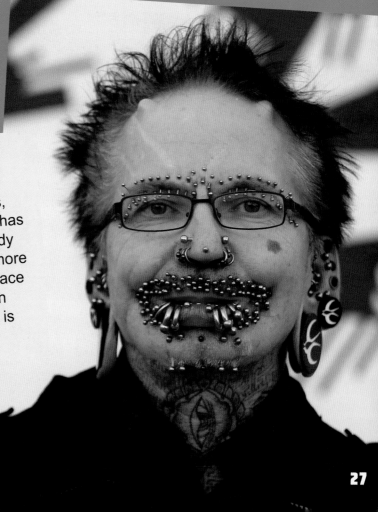

LARGEST GAME OF MUSICAL CHAIRS

The world's largest game of musical chairs took place in 1989 at the Anglo-Chinese School in Singapore. The game started with 8,238 participants and took three and a half hours to finish. The winner was 15-year-old Xu Chong Wei.

LARGEST TOOTHBRUSH CIRCLE

In a toothbrush circle, people stand in a circle and brush the teeth of the person next to them. Camp Kaylie in New York, USA, holds the record for the largest toothbrush circle. In 2013, 126 people brushed one another's teeth at the same time.

LARGEST UNDERWATER WEDDING

The world's largest underwater wedding took place at Jaworzno, Poland, on 27 August 2011. The marriage ceremony was attended by 303 divers and lasted about 18 minutes. The happy couple and the priest communicated using plastic-coated paper and sign language.

MOST PEOPLE HUGGING TREES

In 2013, 951 people gathered at Hoyt **Arboretum** in Oregon, USA, to hug trees. Everyone had to hug trees at the same time for a whole minute. To beat the previous record, organizers asked random visitors to join in the effort. One woman who had just got married hugged a tree in her wedding dress.

arboretum *garden where scientists and other people study different types of trees*

LARGEST TUG-OF-WAR TOURNAMENT

In September 2012, 1,574 students competed in the world's largest tug-of-war **tournament**. The event took place at the Rochester Institute of Technology in Rochester, New York, USA. It was part of the school's annual Mud Tug tournament. More than 150 teams participated. The event raised more than £6,000 for charities.

tournament *series of matches between several players or teams, resulting in a winner*

GOING FOR THE RECORD

Humans are driven to achieve great things. For some people it means running the fastest race or creating a beautiful piece of art. For others greatness comes from underwater knitting or balancing ping-pong balls on their chins. Thousands of people try to break crazy records every year so the rest of us can marvel at their incredible achievements.

GLOSSARY

acrobat person who performs gymnastic displays that require great skill

arboretum garden where scientists and other people study different types of trees

contortionist entertainer who twists his or her body into strange positions

decibel unit for measuring the volume of different sounds

diameter line drawn from one side of a circle to the other, passing through the centre

edible able to be eaten

free fall descend through the atmosphere for a time without the aid of a parachute

genetic relating to physical traits or conditions passed down from parents to children

immersion fully submerged underwater

lisp speech problem that causes a person to incorrectly pronounce certain letters, especially "S" and "Z"

pituitary gland organ that influences many functions in the body, including bone growth

recumbent position in which a person leans back with his or her legs stretched out in front

solar to do with the sun; powered by the sun's energy

tournament series of matches between several players or teams, resulting in a winner

READ MORE

An A-Z of Record Breakers (Project X Origins), Chloe Rhodes (OUP, 2014)

Animal Record Breakers: Fastest, Strongest, Deadliest, Steve Parker (Carlton Books, 2013)

Audacious Aviators: True Stories of Adventurers' Thrilling Flights (Ultimate Adventurers), Jen Green (Raintree, 2014)

WEBSITES

www.ashrita.com
Visit Ashrita Furman's website, (holder of the most Guinness Records at one time), to see photos and video clips of some of his weird and wonderful world records.

www.bbc.co.uk/nature/collections/p00hldcc
Learn about nature's record breakers including the world's smallest primate and the world's longest stick insect.

www.guinnessworldrecords.com
Discover fascinating world records, watch amazing video clips and find out how to set your own world records!

INDEX